# Do It Yourself Projects

## Make Your Own
# Creative Cards

# Rita Storey

**PowerKiDS**
press™

New York

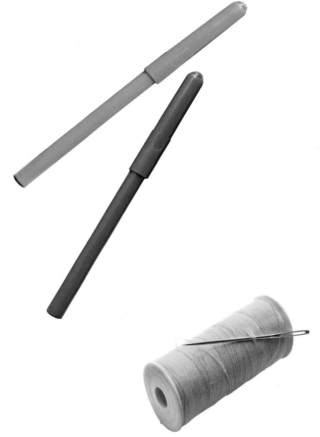

Published in 2011 by The Rosen Publishing Group Inc.
29 East 21st Street, New York, NY 10010

First Edition

Commissioning Editor: Jennifer Sanderson
Packaged for Wayland by StoreyBooks
Project maker: Rita Storey
Photographer: Harry Rhodes—Tudor Photography

Library of Congress Cataloging-in-Publication Data

Storey, Rita.
  Make your own creative cards / Rita Storey.
    p. cm. -- (Do it yourself projects!)
  Includes index.
  ISBN 978-1-61532-591-7 (library binding)
  ISBN 978-1-61532-593-1 (paperback)
  ISBN 978-1-4488-1170-0 (6-pack)
  1. Greeting cards--Juvenile literature.  I. Title.
  TT872.S84 2010
  745.594'1--dc22

                                    2009023754

Photographs:
All photography by Tudor Photography except
page 2 middle I-stock, page 4 KG/Alamy; page 5 top Popperfoto/
Getty Images; page 7 bottom right; page 9 Time & Life Pictures/
Getty Images; page 11 top right; page19 bottom right.

Manufactured in China
CPSIA Compliance Information: Batch #WAS0102PK: For Further Information
contact Rosen Publishing, New York, New York at 1-800-237-9932

### Note to parents and teachers:
The projects in this book are designed to be made by children. However, we do recommend adult supervision at all times as the Publisher cannot be held responsible for any injury caused while making the projects.

# Contents

# All About Cards

A greeting card is a piece of paper or card with a message on it, which is given or sent to another person. Greeting cards are given on special occasions, to say thank you, or even just to say hello.

## CARDS FROM LONG AGO

The Ancient Egyptians and the Chinese sent the very first greeting cards. The Egyptians wrote their messages on a type of paper made from the leaves of a plant called papyrus. The early Chinese people exchanged messages of goodwill at Chinese New Year.

In the mid-1400s, cards began to be printed on paper. The first-known greeting card in existence is a Valentine card made at around this time. It is now on display in the British Museum in London, UK. These early printed cards were very expensive to buy and were delivered by hand.

## NEW TECHNIQUES

In the 1870s, a new printing technique meant that greeting cards could be printed in full color. Since then, handwritten notes and handmade cards have largely given way to mass-produced greeting cards. Pop-up cards, pull-the-tab cards, and turn-the-wheel cards added extra interest to the simple

folded card. Today, the most frequently sent cards are Christmas cards and birthday cards.

## HELP THE ENVIRONMENT

Today, to save energy and help the environment, some people prefer to design their own e-cards on a computer and send them by e-mail. Cards are still sent through the mail, and people often recycle the cards they receive. New cards can be made using the recycled paper.

## GET STARTED!

In this book, you can discover ways of making lots of interesting cards. Try to use materials that you already have either at home or at school. For example, for the cardboard in these projects, the backs of used notepads, art pads, and hardbacked envelopes are ideal. Reusing and recycling materials like this is good for the environment and it will save you money. The projects have all been made and decorated for this book, but do not worry if yours look a little different—just have fun making and giving your cards.

# Printed Card

This card is made using a simple form of block printing. In block printing, patterns are made by printing from blocks with shapes carved into them. Different colors can be printed on top of each other.

**YOU WILL NEED**

sheet of art foam

pair of scissors

cardboard tube

glue or double-sided tape

paint

flat tray

piece of stiff card

newspaper

piece of folded card

**1** Cut simple shapes such as leaves, flowers, cars, or animals from the art foam.

**2** Stick the shapes onto the cardboard tube. Leave about 1⅛ in. (3 cm) without any shapes at each end of the tube.

**3** Put a blob of paint onto the tray. Using the piece of stiff card, spread out the paint into a thin layer.

**4** Roll the cardboard tube along the tray so that the shapes become coated in paint.

**5** Put the folded card onto some newspaper. The side on which you want to print should be facing up. Gently roll the tube over the card so that some of the paint from the shapes prints on the card, but the tube does not touch the paper. Allow your card to dry.

# BLOCK PRINTING

The very first printed books were made using carved wooden blocks. Words and pictures were carved into blocks of wood. Ink was rolled onto the wooden block and the block was pressed onto paper. The blocks could be used over and over again.

# Surprise Card

Christmas cards have always been among the most popular cards. Follow the steps below to make a Christmas card with a hidden surprise.

## YOU WILL NEED

strip of thin red card,
  16½ in. x 2¾ in. (42 cm x 7 cm)
piece of thin yellow card,
  3½ in. x 2⅓ in. (9 cm x 6 cm)
pair of scissors
pencil
2 strips of paper,
  4 in. x ⅖ in. (10 cm x 1 cm)
glue
paintbrush
colored paper

**1** Fold each end of the red card in toward the center, 4 in. (10 cm) from the end.

**2** Turn the card over. Fold it back the other way, 6 in. (15 cm) from each end. Open out the card.

**3** Snip out triangles from the edge of the piece of yellow card to make it jagged. Write the word "Surprise!" on it.

**4** To make the spring, put the ends of the two strips of paper together at right angles. Glue them together.

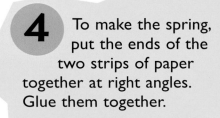

8

**5** Fold the bottom strip over the top strip and crease it. Keep doing this until the paper strips are all folded up.

**6** Brush some glue on the second to the last piece of folded paper and glue the last piece down onto it. Stick the spring in the center of the red card. Glue the yellow jagged card on top of it.

**7** Turn the card over and cut out a triangle shape at the top and bottom of the card on each side, 1¾ in. (4.5 cm) from each end. You now have a rectangular shape with "Surprise!" hidden inside. Decorate the card with colored paper shapes. Fold up the card. As you pull the ends of the card, the "Surprise!" will jump out and wobble.

## CHRISTMAS CARDS

The world's first printed Christmas card was designed in England in 1843 by John Callcott Horsley. More than 2,000 cards were printed and sold that year, which cost a shilling ($6.68 today) each.

# Pop-up Card

For thousands of years, many cultures have used candles to celebrate all sorts of occasions, from birthdays to religious festivals and important ceremonies. You can adapt this candle card to wish them whatever you choose!

**1** Fold the larger piece of card in half. Rub along the fold to crease the card.

**2** Fold the second piece of card in half. Fold the bottom edge up to the top and crease it. Turn the card over and do the same on the other side.

**3** Glue the back of the first and last fold inside the larger folded piece of card to make a right-angled step.

**4** Take the yellow card, and using a ruler and pencil, draw four fat candles on top of a cake. Draw lightly so that you can erase any pencil marks later. Carefully cut around the candles and cake. Take your time, especially around the flames and the edge of the cake.

**5** Cut out four flame shapes from the orange paper. They must be smaller than the yellow flames. Glue the orange flames onto the yellow candle flames. Draw tiny lines with colored glitter glue or a red felt-tipped pen in the center of the flames to look like glowing wicks. Glue the piece of metallic blue paper onto the center of the cake shape.

**6** Glue the candles to the "step" inside your card. Then write your message, outside and inside your pop-up card.

Happy Birthday

# PAPER ENGINEERING

Pop-up greeting cards were very popular in Europe in the late eighteenth century. The technique was developed to be used in pop-up books and adopted to create elaborate Christmas and Valentine's Day cards. A person who designs cards or books with moving parts is called a paper engineer.

# Pull-tab Card

Follow these steps to make your own pull-tab greeting card. By pulling the tab, you can change the clown's expression from sad to happy.

## YOU WILL NEED

- letter sheet of yellow card
- ruler
- pencil
- pair of scissors
- eraser
- double-sided tape
- half letter sheet of white card
- piece of white card, 1⅕ in. x 1½ in. (3 cm x 4 cm)
- colored paper
- glue
- red and black felt-tipped pens
- pieces of colored paper

**1** Fold the card in half along the longest side. On the front of the card, draw two lines 1½ in. (4 cm) from the long edges. Draw one horizontal line 3½ in. (9 cm) from the top of the card and another 3 in. (8 cm) from the bottom of the card. The four points where the lines meet will make a rectangular shape.

**2** Cut out the rectangle from the middle of the card. Erase the pencil lines.

**3** Use double-sided tape to stick together the side opposite the fold and the bottom edge of the card.

**4** Glue the small piece of white card to the top of the larger piece to make a tab. Slide the white card inside the yellow card. Cut out colored shapes and glue them onto the front of the card to make a clown face like the one in the picture. Draw a sad mouth in the rectangle onto the white card.

**5** Using the tab, pull up the white card so that you can no longer see the sad mouth shape. Draw a happy mouth shape onto the white card. Push the white card back inside the card so that the sad mouth is showing.

## CLOWN MAKEUP

White-faced clowns are what most people think of when they think of circus clowns. Every clown creates his or her own face makeup design. Once a clown starts to use a design in their performances, no other clown is allowed to copy it.

**6** Pull the tab at the top of the card to make your clown smile. Your friends will smile, too, when you send them this card.

# Padded Card

In the early 1800s, Valentine cards were made by hand. The cards were made using lace, silks, and satins. Popular designs for these cards were hearts, roses, and pictures of Cupid. Follow the steps below to sew your own Valentine card.

## YOU WILL NEED

piece of colored card,
  12 in. x 6 in. (30 cm x 15 cm)
piece of paper,
  4⅓ in. x 4⅓ in. (11 cm x11 cm)
pencil
pair of scissors
2 pieces of colored felt, each
  4⅓ in. x 4⅓ in. (11 cm x11 cm)
pins
2 smaller pieces of felt in
  different colors
needle and thread
cotton balls
glue
ribbon

**1** Fold the card in half along the longest side.

**2** Fold the paper in half and draw half of a heart shape. Cut around the shape. Unfold it so that you have a whole heart shape.

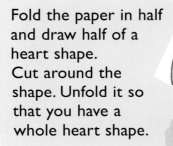

**3** Put the two larger pieces of felt together and pin the paper heart onto them. Cut around the shape.

**4** Unpin the paper heart from the felt and fold it in half again. Draw half of a smaller heart shape inside the first one. Cut it out and unfold it.

**5** Pin the smaller paper heart onto one of the smaller pieces of felt and cut around it.

**6** Follow steps 4 and 5 again, this time making an even smaller heart shape.

**7** Using a running stitch (see panel), sew the two biggest heart shapes together. Before you sew all the way around the shape, push a small piece of the cotton ball into the heart.

# RUNNING STITCH

To sew running stitches, thread a needle and tie a knot in the end of the thread. Push the needle through from the back of the fabric, and pull the thread until the knot stops it from going any farther. Then push the point of the needle back through the front of the fabric, just in front of where the thread has come through. Pull it to make a stitch.
To make a row of running stitches look really good, keep the stitches and the spaces between them all the same length.

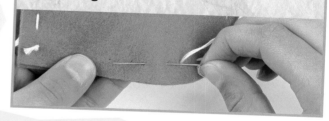

**8** Finish off the stitching by doing the last stitch twice. Push the needle down through the fabric to the back.

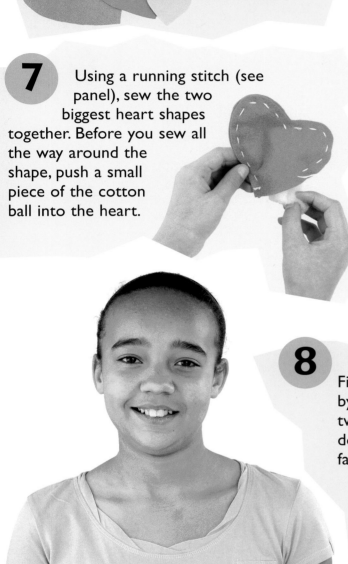

**9** Stick the big remaining heart onto the padded heart. Glue the small heart on top. Put glue on the back of the padded heart and stick it onto the card. Decorate the card with a neat ribbon bow and felt hearts.

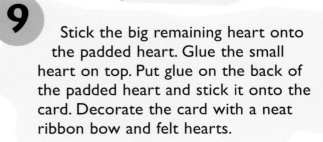

# Photo Card

A card with a disk that moves around can be used to display your favorite photographs. You can use this type of card for any occasion.

**1** Fold the bigger piece of rectangular card in half to make a square.

**2** Open out the compass to 2¾ in. (7 cm) wide.

**3** Draw a circle on the square piece of card and cut it out. Using the point of the compass, make a small hole in the center of the circle.

**4** Place the circle on the front of your folded card. Move it to the right so that the edge of the circle sticks out over the right-hand side of the card by ⅖ in. (1 cm). Make a mark with a pencil through the hole in the middle of the circle onto the card below. Take off the circle.

**5** Close the compass up to ¾ in. (2 cm) wide. Draw a circle on the folded card so that the edge of the circle is ¾ in. (2 cm) from the top and ¾ in. (2 cm) from the right-hand edge.

**6** Cut out the circle.

**9** Draw around the hole in the front of the card onto the wheel underneath. Move the wheel around until you cannot see the pencil lines. Draw around the hole again. Keep moving the wheel and drawing around the hole in the front until you have used up all the space on the wheel.

**7** Push the point of the paper fastener through the front of the folded card where you made the pencil mark (see step 4).

**8** Push the point of the paper fastener through the middle of the circle of card. Open out the paper fastener.

**10** Take the paper fastener out of the card. Put a photo or picture under the cut-out circle on the front of the card and draw around it. Cut it out. Cut out as many photos and pictures as you have circles on the wheel. Stick the photos and pictures onto the circles on the wheel.

**11** Put the card back together with the paper fastener. Decorate the front of the card. Turn the wheel to display your pictures.

# Origami Card

Origami is the Japanese art of paper folding. "Ori" means folding and "kami" means paper in Japanese. Follow the steps below to make an origami boat to go inside a card.

## YOU WILL NEED

piece of colored origami paper, or other colored paper, 5 in. x 6 in. (12.5 cm x 15 cm)

piece of colored card, 8¼ in. x 6 in. (21 cm x 15 cm)

scraps of shiny blue and yellow paper

pair of scissors

glue

paintbrush

**1** Fold the piece of origami paper in half along the longest side. Fold the top corner of the folded side into the middle of the bottom edge like a triangle. Leave a border at the bottom.

**2** Do the same with the top corner on the opposite side, making sure that the edges meet exactly.

**3** Fold the bottom edge of the paper upward.

**4** Turn it over and do the same on the other side.

**5** With your thumb and forefinger, hold the middle of the front of the shape and the middle of the back of the shape and pull it gently into a square.

**6** Press the shape flat.

**7** Take one of the bottom corners of the square and fold it upward. Turn over the paper and fold the other corner in the same way. You now have a folded triangle.

**8** With your thumb and forefinger, hold the middle of the front of the shape and the middle of the back of the shape and pull gently. Press the shape flat, making a square.

**9** Fold the colored card in half, making a firm crease. Cut out wave shapes from the shiny blue paper and a yellow circle for the Sun. Glue these onto the inside of your card. Write your message.

**10** Gently pull the outer corners of the square to unfold your boat. Paint a thin line of glue along the length of the bottom of the boat. Glue the shape onto the inside of the card. Fold the shape flat. The person you give the card to can unfold the boat and float it on the sea.

Happy Father's Day

## ORIGAMI

The art of origami is to make objects, such as animals, birds, and flowers, by folding a single piece of paper. It is possible to make very intricate designs in this way. Some designs even have moving parts, such as birds with wings that flap.

# Glowing Card

Today's greeting cards come in all shapes and sizes. Some cards make noises, play music, or light up when you open them. Follow these instructions to make a card in the shape of a tree with a glowing light at the top.

**1** To make a stand for your tree, measure 3 in. (8 cm) along the long piece of card. Make a mark. Measure a further 1⅛ in. (3 cm) and make another mark. Do the same again.

**2** Make a fold in the card at each mark and tape the ends to make a box shape.

**3** Fold the paper in half and draw half of a Christmas tree in a pot, on the folded edge. Cut out the shape and use it as a pattern.

**4** Using the pattern, draw a tree shape on stiff card. Cut it out. Do the same with the green paper. Glue the green paper onto the card.

20

**5** Glue the box onto the back of the tree at the bottom. Make a hole near the top of the tree. The hole must be large enough for the bulb to fit into it.

**6** Decorate the front of the tree with cut-out paper shapes. Cut a star shape for the top of the tree. Cut a hole in the middle of the star the same size as the hole in the card. Stick the star onto the card.

**8** Attach the crocodile clips to the connectors on either side of the battery holder. The bulb will light up. Take off one clip.

**7** Attach the crocodile clips on one end of each connector to each side of the bulb holder. Push the light bulb gently through the hole.

**9** Put the battery inside the box at the back of the tree. Move the wires so you cannot see them from the front. Reconnect the last wire to light up the tree just before you give it away.

# CIRCUITS

To make the bulb light up, the electric current has to be able to flow from the battery to the light bulb and back to the battery again. This is called a circuit.

# Glossary

**connector**
A device for connecting one object to another.

**crocodile clips**
Long clips that when opened look like the mouth of a crocodile.

**Cupid**
The son of the goddess Venus. Cupid is often pictured on Valentine cards shooting a bow and arrow to help people fall in love.

**e-card**
A card designed on a computer and sent to people by e-mail. Many people send e-cards because they save on postage and paper, which is good for the environment.

**electric current**
The movement of electrical energy around an electric circuit.

**environment**
Everything that surrounds us on the Earth.

**intricate**
Something that has lots of different parts. For instance, intricate origami has a lot of folds.

**mass-produced**
To produce or manufacture goods in large quantities, especially by machinery.

**origami**
The traditional Japanese art of folding paper into animal or flower shapes.

**pattern**
Anything made or designed to be copied many times. For example, a sewing pattern.

**printing techniques**
Different ways of making prints. Block printing is just one of many ways of making a print.

**recycle**
To recycle something is to change it or treat it so that it can be used again.

## reusing

Using something for a different purpose. For instance, if you use cardboard from a cereal box to make a project, you are reusing cardboard.

## shilling

A type of coin that was used in Britain. It would be equal to about $6.68 in U.S. money today.

## tab

A small strip or flap that sticks out. Sometimes tabs are pulled to reveal something that is hidden.

## Valentine

Someone you like or love, to whom you send a card or love token on St. Valentine's day, February 14.

## white-faced clowns

Clowns who apply white makeup all over their face before painting on other colors around the eyes, nose, and mouth.

# FURTHER INFORMATION AND WEB SITES

## BOOKS TO READ

**Greeting Card Making: Send Your Personal Message**
by Deborah Hufford
(Capstone Press, 2005)

**Making Cards**
by Fiona Watt
(Usborne Books, 2007)

## WEB SITES

Due to the changing nature of Internet links, PowerKids Press has developed an online list of Web sites related to the subject of this book. This site is updated regularly. Please use this link to access this list: http://www.powerkidslinks.com/diyp/cards

# Index